GREAT JEWS
SINCE BIBLE TIMES

FOR YOUNG PEOPLE

BY

ELMA EHRLICH LEVINGER

AUTHOR OF

"Bible Stories for Very Little People"
"My Confirmation", "Our Marriage", etc.

BEHRMAN HOUSE, Inc.

PUBLISHERS • NEW YORK

EIGHTH EDITION • 1945

To

SAMUEL H. LEVINGER, who "likes all kinds of history"
this volume of Great Jews Since Bible Times
is affectionately dedicated
by
His Mother

Preface

This collection of Stories of Great Jews Since Bible Times is designed to follow the author's Bible Stories for Very Little People, in both the historical and educational order.

This is simply a book of stories, stories related to the great names of post-Biblical Jewish history, in order that the Jewish child may learn in the easiest and pleasantest way of some of the great men of his people, even before he is ready to study formal history.

In selecting from the great mass of available material the few tales for this volume, the author has always tried to select men with a story attached to their names, even though that meant omitting many others equally important. Perhaps some of these other heroes may be included in another volume, a study of the Rabbis of Israel.

No living men have been included; while in several fields, especially that of philanthropy, it has been necessary to use only a few names to avoid an impression of repetition. The material used is practically all historical, though now and then legends which tradition has connected with some of the great lights of Israel were the only stories available for our purpose. For in every case our choice has been guided by the answer to the childish question: Is it a story?

ELMA EHRLICH LEVINGER.

Columbus, Ohio, July, 1926.

CONTENTS

THE DOOR-KEEPER CARRIED HILLEL INTO THE SCHOOL-ROOM

Hillel, the Poor Student

Hillel was a little Jewish boy whose family had lived in Babylon for many years. When Hillel grew up he wanted to go far-away to Jerusalem because he had heard of the fine Jewish schools there, and was sure that in Jerusalem he could learn more than at home.

Hillel's parents were very poor; they had no money to give him to make the long journey to Jerusalem. After he reached there he had to work very hard every day as a wood-cutter; he spent half of the money he earned for food and a place to sleep; the other half he gave to the door-keeper of the school, that he might get permission to go in and study with the other students.

One day Hillel did not earn as much as usual. Because he could not pay, the door-keeper would not let him enter the school. But Hillel was determined not to lose his lessons for even a single day. He climbed up to one of the high window-sills and settled himself there. He leaned against the window and listened to the words of the Torah which the rabbis taught the students.

Soon it began to snow. Outside, on the window-sill, Hillel shivered from the cold and pulled his ragged cloak closer around him; but he did not want to go home until the day's lessons were over. Inside of the schoolroom it grew very dark. 'At first the teachers thought' it was because of the snow storm. Then one of the students pointed to the one window through which no daylight came at all. The door-keeper went outside to find out what was the trouble. He was very much frightened when he found Hillel there, almost covered with snow. The poor boy was half frozen. He had fainted and fallen against the window.

The door-keeper carried Hillel into the schoolroom. Some one lighted a fire; some one else prepared a hot bath.

After Hillel was undressed and bathed, several of the rabbis rubbed him with sweet-smelling oils and dressed him in comfortable garments.

Then the rabbis asked Hillel why he had hidden himself upon the window-sill. Before he could answer, the door-keeper told the whole story. Now the door-keeper was sorry and ashamed that he had driven Hillel away from the school. He asked Hillel to forgive him.

The rabbis decided that a boy who loved learning so much should not be kept out of their school because he happened to be poor. They told him he would be welcome to come every day without paying any admission fee at all. So Hillel studied for a long time in Jerusalem. He studied so hard that in time, instead of being known as Hillel the Poor Student, he became famous as Hillel the Great Teacher. You will read more about him and his teachings some day in the Stories of the Talmud.

Herod, the Builder of the Temple

Do you know who built the great Temple at Jerusalem? Yes, King Solomon built the first Temple and it was one of the most beautiful buildings the world had ever seen; but a people called the Babylonians made war upon Jerusalem and left the Temple in ruins.

Many years later when Herod was king over Judah he wanted to rebuild the Temple. Herod admired the Romans who were great builders and who erected many wonderful Temples to their gods. And so he too built many marble palaces in Jerusalem, and baths and circuses, and laid out many fair gardens. Then he decided to build a Temple in honor of the God of Israel, although it is very likely that he thought more of honoring himself and astonishing the whole world by the wonderful buildings in his kingdom.

There is a story that Herod built the

10

Temple upon the advice of a Jewish scholar named Baba. Herod, who was one of the cruelest kings who ever lived, had killed a number of Jewish teachers. He allowed Baba to live, but ordered his eyes to be put out. When Baba was blind, Herod came to him, and, pretending to be a poor Jew, spoke to the wise old man of the king's wicked deeds.

"Why do you not curse the king that God may punish him for his wickedness?" asked Herod, just to see what Baba would say.

"Our religion forbids us to curse the king or wish him harm," answered Baba. And although Herod had caused him so much suffering, Baba would not wish him evil.

Then Herod told Baba who he really was. "I am sure that the other rabbis were also good and wise," said Herod, "and I am sorry I had them put to death. How can I make up for all the cruel things I did to them?"

"O King Herod," Baba answered him,

"the wise men and the teachers of the Torah are the 'light of Israel.' When you killed them you put out the light. But you can cause the light to shine again. Rebuild the Temple which will be a Light for the whole world."

So Herod rebuilt the Temple and it became a saying that a man who had not seen the Temple of Herod at Jerusalem had never seen anything really beautiful. Herod was very proud of his Temple, but it did not bring him happiness. He had been a cruel and wicked king and he knew that every Jew despised and feared him.

For, in spite of the Temple which Herod built, every Jew remembered all his terrible deeds, especially his crimes against the teachers and wise men of Israel. So that when Herod died, every man in Jerusalem rejoiced that he no longer sat upon the throne to plan evil against the Jewish people.

REBUILD THE TEMPLE WHICH WILL BE A LIGHT FOR THE
WHOLE WORLD

13

The Wicked Emperor and the Good Philosopher

A philosopher is a man who loves wisdom. No philosopher ever loved wisdom more than Philo of Egypt. He was one of the Jews who had settled in the old Egyptian city of Alexandria; his family was rich and respected; all his friends spent their days in pleasure and merry-making. But Philo was too fond of study to waste his time. Although he was a rich man, he lived like a poor man, wearing plain clothes and eating plain food; he spent his days and nights in study.

Philo hated to leave his books. But when some of his Jewish friends told him that they were going to Rome to see the wicked emperor Caligula, he was willing to go with them and plead for his people. Caligula had done many wicked and foolish things and everyone hated him and feared him. Now the Jewish

people did not know what to do, as the
emperor had given orders for them to
place his statue in their synagogues and
worship it as a god.

"We will die first," said the Jews of
Egypt. "How can we worship anyone
but the God of our fathers? And how
can we bow down to any statue?"

The little party of Jews reached Rome.
At last they were taken into the emperor's presence. Caligula was talking
to some of his slaves. At first he pretended not to notice them. Then he
turned his wicked, stupid face toward
the Jews who had come from Egypt and
said angrily:

"You are foolish men to worship a god
that you cannot see. All my other subjects have accepted me as their god.
Why will you still refuse to give me the
honors that are due a god?"

Philo was not afraid of the angry emperor. He answered him as one speaks
to a foolish, cross child. "Your Jewish
subjects are all true and obedient," he

said. "We have already made three of-
ferings in our synagogue in your honor."

The emperor snarled back at him.
"Yes, sacrifices in my honor! You gave
these honors for me, not to me. You
honor your foolish god but you do not
honor me, your emperor. I have been
too gentle with the Jews. Unless you
worship the statues of my godly self that
I will put up in your synagogues, you
will all be put to death?"

Before Philo could answer him, the
emperor turned away and began talking
to his slaves again. Now and then he
turned back to Philo and the other Jews
to speak to them mockingly; before
Philo could defend his religion, Caligula
would laugh mockingly and pretend not
to listen. Philo shook his head sadly
and whispered to the other Jews to remain silent. He was a wise man, and he
knew it would be foolish to try to con-
vince a fool.

"We have done all we can," Philo
told his friends when the emperor

THE WICKED EMPEROR AND THE GOOD PHILOSOPHER

dismissed them at last.

"Yes," answered one of the Jews of Alexandria. "Now if our God does not help us and protect us from the emperor, we must prepare ourselves to die for Him."

But the Jews were not to suffer much longer from the cruelty of Caligula. Some Roman courtiers whom he had insulted killed him in his own palace. Freed from their tyrant the Jews' of Alexandria had a great festival in which they thanked God for saving them from their enemy. But Philo was not with them; he was already back with his books, which he loved so much, and which he never left again.

———•—■—•———

The Pen and the Sword

An old saying tell us: "The Pen is Mightier than the Sword." Josephus was a Jew who did much more for his people with his pen than with his sword.

Josephus was born in Jerusalem and came from a family of priests. As a boy he was well taught in the Jewish Law; but when he became a young man he went to the great city of Rome. There he saw how powerful the Romans were; he knew they were the masters of the whole world. This made him look down upon his own people.

By the time Josephus returned to Jerusalem the Jews were ready to make war against Rome. Josephus told them that they would never win, for he knew how strong the Roman army was, the strongest in the whole world. But when the Jews would not listen to him he promised to help them fight against Rome.

Josephus was not a coward; but he was not a good soldier. From the beginning he felt that the Jewish soldiers who were placed under his command could not win the war. When he and some of his soldiers were surrounded by the enemy, the soldiers killed themselves rather than fall alive into the hands of the Romans. But Josephus decided to surrender.

The Roman general Vespasian was very kind to Josephus. He gave him riches and made him a member of his own household. After the Romans captured Jerusalem and returned home, Josephus went back to Rome with Vespasian and his son Titus.

But although Josephus had not served his country well with his sword, his pen was more faithful to the Jewish people. Now that the Romans had defeated them in battle, these proud people despised the Jews more than ever, and thought of them as cowards and slaves. So Josephus began to write his famous history, "The

SO JOSEPHUS BEGAN TO WRITE HIS FAMOUS HISTORY

21

Jewish Wars," which is read to this very day.

In his book Josephus showed that the Jews were as brave as any people on earth. He explained that the Romans had conquered and taken Jerusalem because of their greater and larger armies; he said that instead of blaming the Jews for losing the war, they should be praised for holding out so long against such a terrible enemy.

Later, Josephus wrote another book, "Against Apion." Apion was a Greek who had written many wicked lies about the Jewish people. The Greeks and Romans had believed these lies; now Josephus proved how untrue they were. It was a brave book to write, for now Josephus was living among the Romans who might have liked him better if he had forgotten his people and not tried to defend them. But Josephus was always ready to take up his pen to fight for the truth.

It must have made Josephus happy in

his last years to think how he had aided his people with his pen, even if they despised him for throwing away his sword in their defense. But he must have felt sad, too, and a little ashamed, when he realized how many of his countrymen had died fighting with their swords in their hands, and how many of them now lived weary lives as slaves, while he held an honored place in the court of the enemy.

The Burning Torch

When the Roman soldiers captured
Jerusalem, one of them threw a burning
torch into the Temple which Herod had
built. In a short time the beautiful build-
ing was in ruins. The Jews whom the
Romans had not killed in battle, stood
by in chains; they cried aloud in their
sorrow as they saw their Temple disap-
pearing before their eyes.

But Jochanan ben Zaccai did not
weep. When those about him mourned
and said: "The Light of Israel has gone
out forever," he only smiled.

Jochanan ben Zaccai was one of the
wisest of all the wise rabbis of Palestine.
When he knew that the city of Jerusalem would surely be captured by the
Romans, he had himself taken secretly
to the Roman general Vespasian. He
bowed low before the great soldier and
recited the old Jewish prayer which is

24

**Jochanan Ben Zaccai Bowed Low Before The
Great Soldier**

always pronounced when one greets a king or emperor.

"But I am not an emperor," said Vespasian, wondering at his words.

At that moment, a messenger, dust-covered and weary, rode into the camp, flung himself before Vespasian, and hailed him as emperor! He had ridden all the way from Rome to tell Vespasian that the people there had chosen him for their ruler.

Then Vespasian wanted to reward Jochanan ben Zaccai, who, he believed, had been wise enough to foretell his good fortune. "I will grant you anything you ask," he said to the rabbi, "but I will not spare the city of Jerusalem."

"But you will surely spare the little town of Jabneh," answered Jochanan, "and allow the Jewish scholars to visit me there in peace and safety?"

Vespasian knew there was no fort at Jabneh; he knew also that the leading Jewish soldiers were either dead or bound with chains. So he was glad to grant the rabbi what he had asked.

Jochanan went to Jabneh and opened a little school there. In time, the wisest and best of the Jewish scholars came to him that they might all study the Torah together. As they studied the word of God, they stopped grieving so much for the loss of their Temple.

"The Light of Israel did not cease to burn when the Temple was destroyed," said the rabbis, "for the Torah is also a light. As long as we study it and teach it to our children, no one, not even the strong Romans, can hurt the Jewish people."

This is the way Rabbi Jochanan ben Zaccai saved the Jewish people. For when the Temple was taken from them, he carried the torch of learning to Jabneh, preserving the Torah, which is the most precious treasure of the Jewish people to this very day.

———•••———

Akiba, the Peaceful Soldier

Although the Roman soldiers captured the city of Jerusalem and burned the Temple to the ground, many of the Jewish people would not obey them and give up their religion. Just as the soldiers, led by the last of the Jewish captains, Bar Cochba, fought the enemy on the battlefield, the peaceful rabbis in their schoolroom, taught the Torah to their pupils, and refused to bow to the Roman gods.

Akiba ben Joseph was one of the wisest and best-loved of all the Jewish teachers. Although he was a gentle man and a lover of peace, he felt that he could not obey the Roman rulers when they ordered the rabbis to close their schools and cease their teaching of the Torah.

One day a friend, Pappus ben Judah, visited Akiba. Pappus ben Judah was very much afraid of the Romans; he had

28

PAPPUS BEGGED AKIBA TO STOP TEACHING THE TORAH

given up his own religion because they had told him they would put him to death if he remained a Jew. Now Pappus begged Akiba to stop teaching the Torah and to stop obeying the Jewish laws. "If you do not obey the Romans they will surely kill you," said Pappus.

But Akiba only laughed. He told Pappus this fable:

A fox was walking on the banks of a little brook. He saw a number of fishes in the water and wished they would come upon the shore that he might eat them. So the fox spoke kindly to the little fishes.

"Little fishes," said the fox, "don't you know that the wicked fishers have spread nets in the water to catch you. You would be much safer up here upon the dry land."

But the little fishes were just as clever as the fox. "Thank you, kind sir, for your warning," they answered. "But if we are not safe here in the water where we have always lived, how can we ever manage to escape danger upon the land?"

"And the moral of my little fable is this," went on Rabbi Akiba. "The Jews are like the fish, and the Torah and the religion of their fathers is their only home. If we are not safe when we are obeying God and living in our own home, what will happen to us upon the strange shore where the Roman fox is waiting ready to eat us up? That is why it is much safer for the Jews to obey God rather than the wicked Romans."

And so Akiba continued to teach the Torah until the Romans put him to death. The Romans could not understand why he was so brave and happy when he died, but he told them: "All my life I have taught my pupils to love God. Now I know what it really means to love the Lord my God with all my heart, with all my soul, and with all my might."

Then Rabbi Akiba died as bravely as he lived, and the pupils that he had taught carried on his teachings.

Bar Cochba, the Son of a Star

Do you know why the Jewish people called their last brave captain against Rome, Bar Cochba? Because that name means, "the Son of a Star." In those days after the Temple was burned to the ground by the Romans, it seemed to the Jewish people in Palestine that they were wandering about in a dark night, just like little frightened children who are lost and cannot find their way home. Then it seemed to them that a star rose in the sky to give them light and hope.

Bar Cochba was their star. He was a brave fighter, a strong soldier. Many stories are told of his great strength. It is said that even his soldiers were so strong that they could ride through a forest, bend over, and pull up a strong cedar tree as they passed. Jews from all over the country forgot their fear of the Roman armies and came to Bar Cochba,

32

BAR COCHBA

begging him to lead them in battle.

Rabbi Akiba believed in Bar Cochba too, and prayed that he might be the leader God had long ago promised to send to free Israel. He blessed Bar Cochba and prayed that he might drive the Romans out of the land of Palestine forever.

For a while Bar Cochba was very successful in battle. Even the Romans, who were the best-trained soldiers in the world, feared him. The Jews began to hope that they might be free once more.

It all happened so long ago that we are not sure just what Bar Cochba did that his Jewish followers stopped believing in him. Little by little Bar Cochba's men found it harder to escape from the Romans through the underground tunnels, which the soldiers used in those days, when they did not feel strong enough to meet the enemy in battle. People began to tell stories against Bar Cochba; that he had sinned against God and that God had not really chosen him to save the Jewish people from the Romans.

And perhaps Bar Cochba too, began to lose courage, and wonder whether he would really be able to drive the Romans out of Palestine. But he never stopped fighting, until at last, he fell in battle, and the Jews knew that their last great defender could not help them any more.

Many Jews were killed by the victorious Romans, many more were dragged away and sold as slaves. There did not seem to be any more hope for the Jewish people. They felt they would never return to their dear land of Palestine again. They grieved for the loss of their homeland and their beautiful Temple; they grieved, too, for Bar Cochba, the Son of a Star, who could never bring them hope or courage again.

The Rabbi and the Emperor

Rabbi Judah was sometimes called Judah the Prince, not only because he came from the family of King David who had ruled long ago in Israel, but because he was the leading rabbi of his own day. He was born on the very day Akiba died, which people took to be a sign that there would be another great teacher in Palestine to take the place of the one who had just been killed by the Romans.

When Judah grew up he became a very great scholar; he finished collecting the Mishna, a collection of Jewish laws, which Hillel had begun and Akiba had added to. The Mishna is part of the Talmud, one of the most important of all Jewish books.

Judah the Prince was admired and loved not only by the Jews but by the Romans. Even the Emperor Antoninus was his friend. It is said that they used

SPICE OF THE SABBATH MEAL

to meet secretly in an underground room to which the Emperor would come by underground passages from his own palace. There they would sit and talk of many things.

One Sabbath day the rabbi set a feast before the Emperor. But because it was the Sabbath day and the Jews lit no fires upon that day, all of the food was cold. The Emperor ate heartily and seemed to enjoy everything he ate.

The next week the rabbi invited the Emperor to another feast. Now because it was a week-day the rabbi ordered his servants to serve everything hot and steaming from the kitchen. They brought the food to the table in covered dishes that it might still be hot when placed upon the Emperor's plate. It was a long feast and Rabbi Judah was sure that the Emperor would enjoy it.

But the Emperor did not eat so heartily as before. He left most of his food upon his plate. When the last dish was carried away, he turned to the rabbi and said:

"Usually I like hot food and dislike cold. Yet today, when you serve me with food hot from the kitchen and it is placed steaming upon my plate, I do not care for it, while the food you gave me last time, although it was served cold, was the most delicious I have ever tasted. What wonderful spices did you use to make it so appetizing?"

Judah the Prince smiled. "My Emperor," he answered, "my servants sprinkled the food with the spice of the Sabbath."

"The spice of the Sabbath?" cried the Emperor. "What spice is that? Have your cooks bring me some and I will make each of them as wealthy as a king."

"No earthly king can enjoy the spice of the Sabbath," Rabbi Judah told him, "unless he is a Jew. For the spice of the Sabbath is really the joy the Jew feels when he celebrates his Sabbath day; then, even the simplest food tastes delicious to him. How I wish I could teach you to enjoy the spice of our Sabbath."

But although the Emperor loved and admired Rabbi Judah very much, it is not at all certain that he became a Jew. So all his life he must have wished to have had another meal as good as the one Rabbi Judah had prepared for him that Sabbath.

The Boy from Egypt

You all know the story of how Joseph
the Jewish boy went to Egypt and became a prince of Pharaoh's court. But
today I want to tell you about a boy who
came from Egypt, where he was born in
the city of Fayum, and went to live in
Babylon.

His name was Saadiah ben Joseph.
While still young he had gone to Palestine to study, just as Hillel had in the
olden days. Then he made a journey
to Babylon where the great Jewish
Academy had been built at Sura hundreds of years before. Here some of the
greatest Jewish scholars in the world
gathered to study the Torah. Saadiah
was very glad to study quietly among
them. But before long even the leading
rabbis at Sura knew that the boy from
Egypt was the wisest of them all.

And so, although he was from another
country and very young, they appointed

him Gaon. The Gaon was the president or head of the Academy. This was the very greatest honor that could come to any Jew. For now the Jewish people no longer had a Temple of their own with priests serving before the altars; and now they had no armies of soldiers to defend their land, because they were no longer a people with a land of their own.

They had become a nation of scholars who, instead of serving in the Temple, studied and taught the Laws of God, and instead of fighting on the battlefield, wrote long and learned books. The Gaon was considered the general over these soldier-scholars; he was the mightiest man among all the Jews.

Although he loved peace, Saadiah Gaon loved what he thought was the truth even more. He could not agree with a certain leader among the Jews, who had him driven out of Sura. For a number of years Saadiah was not allowed to return to the city where he had

SAADIAH WENT TO LIVE IN BAGDAD

been so happy and successful in his work. But he was not idle; in the fairy-like city of Bagdad, where so many of the Arabian Night stories began, Saadiah continued to study and write, feeling sure that in the end his old enemy would call him back to his work at Sura. And at last he did! He was allowed to go back to Sura and take up his work as Gaon again.

It would take too long to tell you the names of all the books he wrote, but I must mention one very important work —his translation of the Bible. At this time there were many Jews who no longer knew Hebrew and could not understand the Bible. Saadiah Gaon wrote the Bible for these Jews in Arabic, which they could understand and read.

In this way many people of the Mohammedan religion were able to read the Jewish Bible too, for Arabic was their language. This helped them to become better friends of the Jewish people.

44

Four Rabbis Who Went to Spain

You remember the very old college at Sura, in Babylon, where Saadiah taught and was famous all over the world for his great learning. After a while it was necessary to get more money for this Academy, and four rabbis left to go to different countries, to ask the Jews to help them keep up the old college. But while they were on the sea they were captured by pirates and taken to the city of Cordova in Spain and sold as slaves.

This happened very often in the old days, and the Jews, no matter how poor they were themselves, always managed to collect enough money to buy their fellow Jews from the pirates. So they bought the four rabbis and set them free; one of them, Rabbi Moses ben Enoch, with his little son, remained in Cordova. No one knew he was one of the wisest rabbis in the world; they thought he was only a poor Jew whom they had saved from slavery.

Rabbi Moses and his little son went at once to the Academy of Cordova, where the Jews sat studying that great book of Jewish laws, the Talmud. They sat in the back of the room and nobody noticed the two strangers in their shabby clothes. Somebody asked a very hard question on the day's lesson, which not even Rabbi Nathan, who was the principal rabbi of that school, could answer.

After everyone else in the schoolroom had tried to answer the question, Rabbi Moses rose in the back of the room, and, bowing to the teacher, asked permission to speak. He said very politely that he thought they were all wrong, even Rabbi Nathan. Then he answered the hard question himself. Rabbi Moses spoke so well and showed so much learning that when he finished speaking every student in the school rose and praised him.

Rabbi Nathan, the teacher, was not

SO THEY BOUGHT THE RABBIS AND SET THEM FREE

47

jealous, for he saw at once that the shabby stranger was a much wiser man than he. He came down from the platform and bowed before the traveler from far away Sura.

"Praised be the Lord our God who has brought the light of learning to our city!" said Rabbi Nathan. "You, O stranger, are a much wiser man than I. I beg that you take my place and teach this school in my stead."

Everybody agreed that Rabbi Moses Ben Enoch should be the Chief Rabbi and teacher of the Academy of Cordova. As soon as he became the head of the school, it grew to be one of the most famous of all the Jewish Academies of Spain.

And the story was repeated with each of the other three rabbis! Wherever they went they were so respected for their learning, that they were asked to remain and become teachers of the Spanish Jews.

They never returned to the Academy

at Sura and soon it was no longer the greatest of the Jewish schools. But the Jewish schools in Spain grew more famous day by day, until Jews all over the world turned to Spain as the center of Jewish learning.

So when the torch of learning died at last in Babylon, it burned more brightly than ever in the schools of Spain.

The Far Away Kingdom

About the time that Moses Ben Enoch taught in the Academy at Cordova, the Jews of Spain learned of a far away Jewish kingdom hidden among the mountains on the borders of Russia. It was made up of Turks, Slavs, Bulgars and other mountain tribes. How had these strange and savage people come to believe in Judaism?

The Chazars, as the people of this Jewish kingdom were called, told this story. Once upon a time their king named Bulan had a wonderful dream. He dreamed that a shining angel came to him and told him not to believe in the many gods of the savage tribes about him, but to believe in One God. Bulan knew that the people of three religions all believed in one God—the Mohammedans, the Christians and the Jews.

Bulan called a priest from each religion to come and explain its teachings to him. First the Mohammedan priest told him all the good things he knew about the religion of Mohammed, his prophet. He also praised Moses, the prophet and teacher of the Jews.

Then the Christian priest explained to King Bulan just why he thought his was the best religion. He also spoke of the Bible of the Jewish people in which every Christian believed.

But the rabbi who spoke for the Jewish religion did not speak of any other prophet or book but his own Torah.

So Bulan called the Mohammedan priest aside and said to him: "After your religion which religion do you consider the best?" The Mohammedan answered promptly: "The Jewish religion, the religion of Moses."

Then Bulan spoke alone to the Christian priest and asked him: "If you were not a Christian, which religion would you prefer?" "The Jewish religion," answered the Christian priest.

And, of course, the Jewish rabbi said his religion was the best.

"I think so, too," exclaimed King Bulan, "for the other two religions which teach the One God are both drawn from your faith. I will accept the teachings of the Jewish religion and my people will also become Jews."

Then the Chazars became Jews and the people were taught the Torah and the Talmud in their schools, and learned the Hebrew language. For a long time they were a strong and powerful people, but at last they lost their power. Their last ruler, King Joseph, went to Spain, and the Chazars were scattered through many countries to mingle among the other Jews.

So today nothing but a story remains of the Far Away Kingdom of the Chazars who became Jews in the time of King Bulan, long ago.

THE RABBI SAID HIS RELIGION WAS THE BEST

How Rashi Saved His People

Rashi, the great Jewish scholar, who wrote so many wise and learned books upon the Bible, lived in France so long ago that we know very little about his life. But there are many stories about him, which may or may not be true. All of these tales show what a noble and great-hearted man the great writer was. Perhaps the finest of these stories is the one telling how Rashi saved his people.

Rashi, while traveling, once met a priest and they became friendly, a very strange thing in those sad times when the Christians and the Jews had not yet learned to be good friends. The priest became ill, and Rashi, who, like so many Jews of his day, was learned in medicine, took care of him and cured him. The priest promised that he would never forget the rabbi's kindness.

Years later when Rashi was visiting in

the city of Prague, all of the Jews of that
city came to greet him and listen to his
words, for by that time he was known
as one of the wisest rabbis in the world.
Rashi was very happy at the honor
shown him.

But in those days a Jew could not be
happy for very long. The Jewish people
were made to pay large sums of money
for taxes; they were forced to live walled
off by themselves in a part of the city
called the Ghetto. Their lives were always in danger, for when bad people
wanted to kill them and take away their
money and their goods, such wickedness
was never punished.

And that is just what happened when
Rashi was preaching and teaching in
Prague. A mob of people who hated the
Jews entered the Ghetto and began to
burn the houses and rob and kill the Jewish men, women and children. Rashi
himself, because he was a stranger, was
thrown into prison.

The bishop, who was the head of all

the Christian priests of Prague, went to
visit Rashi in prison, because he had
heard that the stranger was considered
the wisest Jewish teacher who had ever
come to that city. As soon as he saw
the strange rabbi, the bishop of Prague
threw his arms about the stranger and
kissed him. Yes, you have guessed it;
the great and powerful bishop of Prague
was once the poor and simple priest
whose life Rashi had saved long ago.

"My dear friend," cried the bishop.
"How dared anyone throw you into prison? I will take you to my own palace
at once and you shall be treated as an
honored guest."

"Do not think of me," answered
Rashi. "If I am indeed your friend, just
grant me one reward for the little I may
have done for you years ago in the inn.
You are as powerful as a king, in Prague.
Give orders that no one shall harm the
Jews any longer."

The bishop ordered his soldiers to
hurry to the Ghetto and drive out the

THE BISHOP OF PRAGUE THREW HIS ARMS ABOUT RASHI
AND KISSED HIM

wicked people who had planned to kill all the Jews of Prague. Then he took Rashi with him to his palace and treated him like an honored guest. He wanted Rashi to remain with him for a long visit; but as soon as he could, Rashi returned to the synagogue. There the Jews of Prague loaded him with rich gifts, and when he returned to France, he took with him the fairest of all the Jewish maidens of Prague as his bride.

Pilgrims to Palestine

During the time when Rashi taught and wrote in France, hundreds and hundreds of knights in shining armor, and farmers in rough, short robes, and even little children, might have been seen leaving their homes in Europe on a long and dangerous journey. Each carried a cross or wore one fastened to his sleeve, so the journey they took was called a crusade, which means "cross." And the crusades —there were nine of them in all—led to Palestine.

Ever since they left Egypt, Palestine has been a Promised Land, a Holy Land, for the Jews. Then it became a Holy Land for all the people of the Mohammedan and Christian religions, too. In the days of the Crusades, many many Christians left their homes that they might visit Palestine. Because it was a Holy Land to them, and because they thought of Jerusalem as a Holy City, they wished to drive out the Mohammedans and the Jews.

Not all of the Crusaders were cruel and wicked people. King Richard the Lion-hearted of England even punished some Englishmen who drove all the Jews of York to death. He was as generous and honest as he was brave; no wonder that Saladin, the Sultan of the Mohammedan people, admired and loved him. But many of the kings and the common people who came on the crusades, forgot the teachings of their own religion and did dreadful things to both Jews and Mohammedans just because these people had different religions.

As the crusaders passed through Europe on their way to Palestine they often left burning towns behind them, towns in which every Jew had either been killed or had killed himself rather than fall into the enemy's hands. When they reached Jerusalem, the crusaders seemed to forget that it was a Holy City and that

KING RICHARD, THE LION-HEARTED

its name meant "built in peace," for they turned it into a city of battle and of bloodshed. It is said, that after the Christians of Europe captured Jerusalem, not a Jew or Mohammedan was left alive behind its walls.

It makes us very sad to read of these things; yet we must remember that to the Jew, the crusades did not mean noble knights riding on prancing horses as they set out to do brave deeds. To the people who had first thought of Palestine as a Holy Land, the crusades meant burnt synagogues and ruined homes and the loss of one's parents or children.

But the crusades meant something more to the Jew!

The Jews who lost all they held dear on earth during these dark and bloody days learned to cling closer to God and their Torah, for they knew that not even the armies of the kings who marched to Palestine could take these treasures away from them, while the Jews of Spain and certain parts of France, who had not suffered as terribly as the Jews of Germany and Bohemia and Palestine, were drawn closer to their scattered brethren all over the world. They opened the doors of their houses to these homeless wanderers; they invited them to study in the synagogues which the crusaders had left unharmed.

And as they prayed, every Jewish face turned toward the east—toward Palestine, which had been and which must always be the Holy Land of the Jew, although no Jews dared show themselves at that time within its walls, and strangers held its gates.

At the Gates of Jerusalem

Would you like to hear a riddle which may be new to you, but which is really very old? Judah ha Levi the great Jewish poet wrote it when he lived in Spain, many many years ago. He wrote it in Hebrew, but in English it reads like this:

What is it that's blind, with an eye in its
> head,
But the race of mankind its use cannot
> spare;
Spends all its life in clothing the dead,
But always itself is naked and bare?

Have you guessed the answer? Yes, a needle. Judah ha Levi wrote many of these riddles, as well as other bright and merry verses.

But not all of his poetry is so amusing. He wrote serious religious poems, poems about nature and God, poems for marriages and poems on death. But he wrote most of all about the Jewish people.

For although Judah ha Levi was so happy in Spain where the Jews were then treated very kindly, he was sad when he remembered how cruelly his people suffered in many other countries. What made him saddest of all was the thought that the Jewish people had no country they might call their own; that they were scattered over the whole earth, while the beautiful city of Jerusalem, which had once been their home, was now a heap of ruins. He wrote that if he had the wings of an eagle he would fly back to Jerusalem to weep over the broken stones—all that remained of what had once been so beautiful.

As he grew older he felt he could live no longer without a sight of the Holy Land. It was a long and dangerous journey in those days from Spain to Palestine, but Judah was not afraid. When he reached Egypt, the Jews who lived there begged him to remain as their guest, but he insisted on going on. He could not rest until he stood before the gates of Jerusalem.

Judah wandered on, a pilgrim through many lands. He passed through the cities of Tyre and Damascus, but he would not linger long although he found kindly friends who told him of fresh dangers that lay before him. For many years he had longed to see Jerusalem, the Holy City of David, who had also been a poet of Israel. Judah ha Levi felt he must hurry on his way.

But as he neared the city of Jerusalem, Judah, instead of growing happier that he was at last reaching the end of his journey, became sad. He wondered how it would seem to be a stranger in the city of his fathers. For he knew that Jerusalem now belonged to Christians; while the Mohammedans, who also thought of it as a holy place were always ready to attack pilgrims of another faith.

Still he pressed on, hoping to find and kiss the very stones which mark the place where once the Temple stood. When he came to the gates of the city he fell upon the ground, thanking God that he had

AN ARAB HORSEMAN RODE PAST AND STRUCK JUDAH WITH
HIS SPEAR

come at last within sight of the holy place.

As Judah ha Levi bowed himself to the ground, praying and weeping, an Arab horseman rode past and struck him with his spear. So after all his hopes and his wanderings, Judah ha Levi died before he entered the Holy City, breathing his last as he lay in the dust before the Gates of Jerusalem.

The Happy Traveler

Abraham Ibn-Ezra loved to travel from place to place. He was born in the beautiful old city of Toledo, Spain, in the golden days when Jews were still happy in that lovely land. But Abraham was a restless soul who wanted to see the world.

He traveled from country to country, from city to city. He roamed through Africa, Palestine and Arabia. He studied and taught in Italy, he stayed long enough in England to write a learned book on the Sabbath. Everywhere he went, he studied people and languages and customs; he wrote about them afterwards in the most delightful and interesting way.

His mind was as restless as his body. He was never satisfied to write about just one or two subjects; he wrote a long, clever poem about the game of chess; he wrote lovely religious poems, love poems, many jokes and riddles. And he did well in all he wrote. What could be more beautiful than this simple verse about God:

"I see Thee in the starry field,
I see Thee in the harvest's yield.
In every breath, in every sound,
An echo of Thy name is found,
The blade of grass, the simple flower,
Bear witness to Thy matchless power."

All of Abraham Ibn-Ezra's works were written in Hebrew and were much admired in his day. Perhaps the Spanish Jews loved these verses most for the joyous spirit that filled them, as if they knew that some day the Jewish people would be forced to leave the sunny land of Spain where they had been so happy. For no man ever sang more joyfully than Abraham Ibn-Ezra—even when he knew misfortune.

You see, it was not an easy thing to be a traveler in those days. There were no railroads, no safe and swift ocean liners, and of course, nobody had ever dreamed of an airplane! It was even harder for a Jewish traveler who might be robbed and beaten any moment on the road just because he was a Jew. So to enjoy his travels it was necessary to laugh away all his troubles.

That is just what Abraham Ibn-Ezra did. When he went to Egypt he tried to visit Maimonides the great Jewish doctor and rabbi. Maimonides was too busy to see him. But Abraham was not angry. Instead, he laughed and wrote merrily:

I call on my lord in the morning,
But am told that on horseback he's
    sped;
I call once again in the evening,
And hear that his lordship's abed.
But, whether his highness is riding,
Or whether my lord is asleep,
I am perfectly sure disappointment
Is the one single fruit I shall reap.

Not even being really poor troubled this happy traveler. He said that if he sold clothes for the dead, nobody would die; if he became a candle maker, the sun would shine all night and nobody would need to buy his candles. With such bad luck, he asked, how could a man hope to become rich?

Till the day of his death Abraham Ibn-Ezra traveled through life, laughing at his own troubles, trusting in God. It is said that he died with a joke upon his lips just as though he was happy and eager to travel into a new country he had never seen before.

THE HAPPY TRAVELER

Moses Maimonides, the Good Doctor

Moses Maimonides was just the sort of a doctor you are always glad to have come and see you when you are sick. As soon as he stepped into the sick room, the patient felt better, because the doctor was cheerful and kind; he knew just what medicines to give, but very often he just gave good advice. He would tell sick people that they had been eating too much, or taking too little exercise. He believed that if a man obeyed the laws of health he would seldom be ill or unhappy.

Many of the greatest doctors in the world came to visit Maimonides when he lived in Cairo, Egypt; others wrote to ask his advice. The ruler of Egypt and Palestine, Saladin, one of the most powerful sultans that ever lived, appointed Maimonides as one of the royal physicians, which was a very great honor for anyone, especially a Jew. He admired and trusted Maimonides so much that he praised him to the king of England, who had come on a Crusade to Palestine.

This king was called Richard the Lion-hearted, because of his bravery. Richard wanted to appoint Maimonides as his own physician, but Maimonides refused. Perhaps he did not wish to leave the court of Saladin who had always treated him so kindly; or he may have heard how badly the Jews of England were treated at that time and preferred to live among Saladin's people, who, although they were Mohammedans and did not believe in the Jewish religion, were much kinder to the Jews than any of the Christians of that day.

But although Maimonides had to visit the Sultan's palace every day, he still found time to cure the common people who used to come to him, whenever they were ill, to wait before his house until he came out to treat them. No matter how tired he was, or how poor the patient who came to see him was, Maimonides always gave him the same careful treatment that he gave to the richest and most powerful princes in Saladin's court.

But while Maimonides was so busy with his work as a doctor, he found time to be another kind of a doctor too. He was also a doctor of Jewish law and knew more about the Torah than the wisest rabbis of his day. If he had wanted to, he could have spent all his time in his library, just answering the questions which people from all over the world were always bringing or writing to him.

Maimonides' father was one of the leading Jewish scholars in Spain, where his son was born and lived until he was about thirteen years old. All through their travels until they reached Egypt, the father had taught his son; now in Cairo, after his father's death, Maimonides went on with his studies, not only in the Jewish, but in the Christian and Mohammedan religions as well, until he knew almost as much about these faiths, as his own.

MAIMONIDES WAS THE SULTAN'S DOCTOR

Every night when his many duties as a doctor were over, he used to write the books which are still studied by the rabbis and Jewish scholars of our own day. He became so famous for his learning that often when there was a quarrel among Jewish people, they came to him as judge. People knew that he would not only choose wisely, but would also work for peace. No man ever tried harder to teach the Jewish people that they should all love each other like brothers.

After a long and busy life, Moses Maimonides died in Egypt, the land where Moses, the great Jewish law-giver, had once lived and worked for the Jewish people. That is why there is a Jewish saying: "From Moses (the law-giver) to Moses (Maimonides) there has been no one like Moses."

How Nachmanides Found the Palace of the King

While the Jews were still enjoying the Golden Age of Spain and were well treated there, an old, old man named Nachmanides prepared to go upon a long journey.

Nachmanides like the great Maimonides, who lived before him, was a doctor both of medicine and Jewish law. He was not only a writer upon the Jewish religion but such a fine speaker as well, that when the King of Spain called upon the Jews to explain their religion to him, Nachmanides was chosen to speak for them. For four days this Jewish teacher stood before the King of Spain and explained to him and his Christian priests why the Jewish people preferred to keep their own religion.

The King of Spain was so pleased with Nachmanides and his strong defense of his own religion that he gave him a present; but the priests were angry and finally persuaded the ruler to banish Nachmanides from the kingdom.

Nachmanides was now an old man, over seventy. He had spent all his life in Spain and had thought of himself as a true Spaniard. But now he found himself a hated Jew, driven into strange lands by the very King who had promised to befriend him.

Then Nachmanides remembered that there might still be a home for him in Palestine. There his people had once lived free and happy, serving no King but their God. He felt that although the Temple, the Palace of the King, was in ruins, he might be happy there. Taking his traveler's staff in his hand, the old man bade his friends farewell and journeyed to Palestine.

There he gathered about him a little company of friends who loved him for his goodness and wisdom. True, he sometimes sighed as he thought of the lovely home he had left behind him in

HE FELT REAL HAPPINESS IN VISITING THE RUINS OF
THE TEMPLE

the pleasant land of Spain; of his sons and his daughters he wrote, "my heart will dwell with them forever."

But he was not too lonely. He writes in one of his books that it was a great joy to be in Jerusalem; he felt real happiness in visiting the ruins of the Temple and crying over the stones of the holy place. For although the House of God was no longer a thing of beauty, Nachmanides was glad that his feet had wandered there at last.

He knew he would not have to travel any further in his old age. For, as he says in one of the poems still sung on the Day of Atonement, at last he had found his true home in the Palace of the King.

———•━•———

A Friend at Court

Whenever the Jews who lived under the rule of Isabella and Ferdinand of Spain were in trouble, they thought of Don Isaac Abarbanel, their best friend. He was a proud man who claimed that his family had descended from that best loved king of Israel, David. They had settled in Spain years before and had always served the Spanish kings faithfully and with honor.

Isaac wrote several important books on Jewish subjects, but he best served his people as a statesman, when he defended his people before the government. He was called "a shield and a wall for the race", and leading Jewish scholars and statesmen used to meet in his house. The common people who heard how he had collected money to free some Jews sold as slaves in Morocco, looked upon him as their best friend.

When Torquemada who hated Jews, became powerful in court, he was very angry to find that Isaac Abarbanel had charge of all the money of King Ferdinand and his wife Isabella. But as this wealthy Jew had lent them a great deal of money to pay their expenses in the wars against the Moors, and had always acted with great wisdom and honor in handling their affairs, they would not listen to any charges against him.

Then came the news that all the Jews would be forced to leave Spain unless they gave up their religion. They had lived in Spain for hundreds of years; they felt it was their real home. The Jews had been among the leading merchants and doctors of their adopted country. They felt sure that there was some terrible mistake; that King Ferdinand and the beautiful Queen Isabella would listen if only the proper person spoke for them.

So Don Isaac Abarbanel went to court. At first he pleaded that the Jews

who had always shown themselves good
citizens should be allowed the rights of
other citizens, the privilege of remaining
in their home country. When he saw
that none of his arguments moved the
stubborn king and queen he had served
so well, he offered the immense sum of
thirty thousand ducats as a "gift" to the
monarchs that they might be better able
to carry on their wars against the Moors.

Thirty thousand ducats! A great gift!
Ferdinand's eyes glistened with greed at
the thought; the lovely queen smiled
down upon her Jewish friend. There
was a rustle in the group of courtiers
near the door; through them pushed a
tall, dark figure with a stern, cruel face.
It was Torquemada the priest who was
the real ruler of Spain.

"Will you take this money and give up
your religion?" he cried fiercely. "Is the
gold of the whole world worth anything
if you allow these Jews to remain in our
Christian Spain and turn others to their
own disbelieving religion? Send these

cursed people and their gold forth, or you will be cursed now and for all time to come."

Isabella trembled before him; she thought that she had sinned by thinking even for a moment of disobeying the will of the church; Ferdinand turned to the waiting Jewish statesman. "Take your gold and depart," he cried angrily, "just as your cursed people will depart from my kingdom."

Don Isaac Abarbanel bowed and hurried to the outer court where a group of the leading Jews of Spain waited for his answer. When they saw the grief in his face, they bowed their heads and wept bitterly. For they loved Spain and to them banishment from their beautiful country seemed almost as hard to bear as death.

"Send These Cursed People And Their Gold Forth,"
Torquemada Commanded The Queen

The Wandering People

From the window of his splendid palace, Torquemada looked toward the city's gates. Although he wore simple black robes and there was no gold crown upon his shaven head, this man with the cruel, hard face, was more powerful than even his master, King Ferdinand. For Torquemada was the chief inquisitor of Spain.

As chief inquisitor, Torquemada spent his time in discovering whether the Jews and Mohammedans in Spain were obeying the Christian religion. If he or his officers found out that anybody remained true to his own religion and practiced it in secret, Torquemada would order the man, and sometimes his whole family, to be thrown into prison. There they would be treated very cruelly; often they would be put to death.

But even this did not satisfy the evil heart of Torquemada, and one day he was very happy when he saw that the dreadful plan he had long hoped to see accomplished had at last come to pass.

A little boy, son of one of the palace servants, climbed upon the high, broad window sill.

"Oh, see all these people going down the road!" he cried. "There are hundreds and hundreds of them. There are men with gray beards; they are so old they can hardly walk. And see the little boys, much smaller than I am, whom their mothers have to carry. But what do some of the old men carry in their arms?"

"The scrolls of their Law, which they respect instead of the teachings of our own Holy Church," answered Torquemada and he frowned angrily.

"Who are all these people?" asked the little boy.

"Jews who will not give up their own religion and are therefore being driven from Spain," was the answer. "At last I have persuaded our gracious majesties, King Ferdinand and Queen Isabella, to send them into exile. They have been forced to sell their houses; they have been ordered to leave the homes where they have lived all their lives, and seek a new dwelling place beyond the borders of Spain."

The little boy looked troubled. "I am sorry for the poor people," he said. Then, because he was such a little boy, and soon forgot his sorrow for others, he clapped his hands with joy. "Oh, look," he cried, pointing to the far away harbor, "look at the three ships that are leaving the harbor."

"They are the ships of Columbus," answered the cruel, dark man.

Again the little boy looked at the long, wavering line of men, women, and children who were leaving their fatherland of Spain forever.

"Where will they find a home?" he asked.

Torquemada did not answer. But a sudden ray of sunlight broke through the heavy clouds and fell upon the fair white sails of the flagship of Columbus, setting out to find a new world beyond the sea.

"Who Are All These People?" Asked The Little Boy

How Three Ships Left Spain

When King Ferdinand and Queen Isabella ruled the land of Spain, a sailor named Christopher Columbus came to their court. At that time even the wisest men thought that the earth was flat; but Christopher Columbus had studied the maps and charts of a Jewish map-maker, who believed that the earth was round like a ball. In those days everybody wanted to find a short road to India; now Christopher Columbus decided that if the earth was really round it would be possible to sail across the ocean to find India instead of taking the longer trip by land.

Nearly everybody laughed at Columbus. But one of the priests of Isabella's court believed in his plans and begged Isabella to listen to them. Then Isabella believed in Columbus too and wanted to help him.

But although Isabella was the Queen of Spain she was very poor. There had been many wars in Spain and the treasury where the royal money was kept was quite empty. The court treasurer, Gabriel Sanchez told her that there was not a penny to give Columbus that he might buy ships and hire sailors to go with him to look for India.

Then Isabella took off her glittering necklaces and bracelets and rings. "Take these jewels", she told the treasurer, "and bring me money for them that I may help Columbus sail across the Sea of Darkness which no man has ever crossed before."

Gabriel Sanchez, the court treasurer, was really a Jew. But in those days, the Jews of Spain were treated so cruelly that many of them became Maranos (or Secret Jews) and pretended to be like the Spaniards around them, while they practised the Jewish religion behind closed doors. Gabriel Sanchez believed in Columbus too, and wanted to help him.

So he answered Queen Isabella: "O Queen, keep your jewels, because they are more beautiful on you than they would be on any other lady in the kingdom. And I will try to find enough money for you to help Columbus on his first voyage across the Sea of Darkness."

Then Gabriel Sanchez went to many of his friends, who were also Secret Jews, and asked them for money for the queen. They gave him enough gold to build three ships and hire sailors to go with Columbus. One of his relatives gave a very large sum from his own private fortune.

In the month of August, in the year 1492, three ships left Spain to cross the Sea of Darkness. On the flagship, the Santa Maria, was Columbus, and among his crew were three Secret Jews. It is said that one of them, Luis de Torres, was the first man of the crew to land, which means that he was possibly the first white man who ever stepped upon the shores of America.

But Luis de Torres and the other Jews who were with him did not know that some day America would be the home of many many Jews who would leave their own lands in Europe to find peace and happiness in the new land Columbus had discovered.

QUEEN ISABELLA SAID: "TAKE THESE JEWELS"

95

The Jews Come Back to England

When the Jews were driven from Spain and Portugal, a great many of them went to Holland. The Dutch people treated them very kindly and allowed them to keep their own religion.

Manasseh ben Israel was one of their rabbis. Like so many Jewish scholars and rabbis of olden times, he earned his living by a trade and worked as a printer. It is said that he printed one of the first Hebrew books ever printed in Holland. He not only printed books but he composed them, not in one language, but in five! Many of his books were read not only by Jews but by Christians, as well, who in this way learned to know more of the Jewish people and to respect their religion.

But all of Manasseh's learning did not bring him enough money to take care of his family; he was about to leave Holland for South America, when some wealthy Jews opened a Hebrew school. As the head of this school and the leading rabbi of the Dutch Jews, Manasseh was now able to stop his other work and spend all his time teaching and writing and planning for the Jewish people.

Although the Jews were free and happy in Holland, Manasseh was not satisfied. He was sad to think that in some lands they were badly treated; that some countries would not grant them a home. Manasseh hoped that some day the Jews might be permitted to return to their homeland in Palestine. But he believed that first the Jewish people must be scattered all over the world, just as the Bible foretells they must wander, before they can return home.

In the time of Manasseh there were no Jews in England, for they had all been driven out of that country hundreds of years before, by King Edward the First. So Manasseh made up his mind that they should be allowed to return.

At that time there was no king in England. The country was ruled by the Puritans — Christians who said they wanted a purer and plainer religion, and their leader, who ruled England, was Oliver Cromwell. Oliver Cromwell like all the Puritans believed the Bible. He was much interested in the Jews. When Manasseh came to England and explained to Cromwell that the Bible had foretold the Jews would return to Palestine only after they were scattered through every country in the whole world, Cromwell began to wonder why they were not allowed to live in England.

Manasseh explained to Cromwell that the Jews were not the wicked people the Englishmen of King Edward's time believed them to be. He begged that they should be allowed to return.

Cromwell was willing to have the Jews return to England, but certain people, who were very powerful in the country, refused. So Manasseh went back to Holland, an unhappy and a disappointed man. He died shortly afterwards; had he lived, he would have been glad to know that his work had brought about what he had dreamed of so long— for the Jews were allowed to return to England.

MANASSEH EXPLAINING TO CROMWELL

The Man Who Made Spectacles

Baruch Spinoza lived in Amsterdam, Holland. Manasseh ben Israel was one of his Jewish teachers, and he learned Latin and Greek and German, besides. As he grew older, he began to wonder whether every thing his teachers taught him was true.

Nowadays it is a good thing for a young man to think for himself. But the Jews who lived in Holland in the days of Spinoza did not want people to think for themselves. Before the Jews had come to Holland they had suffered so much for their religion in Spain that their religion became doubly dear to them; they felt that a young scholar should repeat only what the older rabbis taught him and no more. Perhaps because they had been treated so cruelly by the priests in Spain the rabbis of Holland often forgot to be kind and generous.

So when Spinoza said that he did not believe everything that the rabbis taught in the schools, he was driven out of the

Jewish congregation. No Jew was allowed to be his friend any longer.

This must have hurt Spinoza a great deal. He had a kind and loving heart and he wanted to keep his friends. But dearly as he loved many of his Jewish brethren, he loved what he thought to be the truth even more. For the rest of his life he was apart and lonely — but he served the truth.

Besides teaching and writing the books which all scholars, Jewish and non-Jewish, admire today, Spinoza earned his daily bread by cutting lenses for spectacles. It is said that just as the scholars admired his books, so did the makers of spectacles in Amsterdam praise his lenses which were always beautifully made. For Spinoza was a careful worker in all things.

Of all Spinoza's teachings no words are more wise and beautiful than those he spoke to a Christian woman in whose house he lived for the last years of his life.

She was an ignorant woman who was

not able to read any books on religion. Until she knew Spinoza she no doubt thought that the Christian religion in which she believed was the only true religion. Then Spinoza came to live with her family. She had never known any Jews before. She knew nothing of their religion. But she had always thought they were rather a wicked people because they did not go to her church.

She saw how honest Spinoza was in all he did and said; she noticed how polite he was to her and her husband, how generous and kind to her little children. She began to wonder whether his religion was not also a good religion, even if it was different from hers.

"Sir," she said one day, "I have never known a Christian as good as you. Is Judaism a better religion because it makes you such a good man?"

"All religions are good," answered Spinoza, "that lead one to a good life."

The untaught woman understood and was satisfied with his answer.

"All Religions Are Good," Said Spinoza," That Lead
One To A Good Life

The Turkish Messiah

The Jews have always waited for a Messiah. Long ago they hoped that a king from the family of David, whom they loved more than all their other kings, would come and rule over them, drive away their enemies, and bring them happiness and peace. During the dark days of Jewish history when they were driven from country to country, they never stopped hoping for the Messiah who would surely come in time to bring them back to the Holy Land.

Then in the town of Smyrna in Turkey, a merchant had a son whom he called Sabbatai Zevi. This boy as he grew older and studied the books of his people began to dream strange dreams. When he read the Zohar, a book which tells of magic and many wonderful things which some Jews believed happened long ago, he wondered whether he could not bring about wonders for his people. At last he was certain that he was the Messiah sent by God to rescue the Jewish people from

all their troubles and lead them back to
Palestine.

The Jewish people were so unhappy
at that time that many of them were glad
to welcome Sabbatai Zevi. All over
Turkey Jews began to close their shops,
and tell their families to get ready for
the journey to the Holy Land with the
wonderful Messiah as their leader. Soon
the news spread throughout Europe. In
every country Jews believed that their
Messiah had come.

But the Sultan who ruled over Turkey
at that time did not believe that Sabbatai
Zevi was the Messiah. The Sultan was
a Mohammedan. He really did not care
how much the Jews of his kingdom believed in Sabbatai Zevi; but they were
good, hard-working citizens, and he did
not want to see them rushing away from
their homes to follow a man the Sultan
believed would only lead them into
trouble. So he put Sabbatai Zevi in
prison.

Still the Jews did not lose their faith
in him. They said that Sabbatai Zevi
could really work wonders. They waited
for a sign from their Messiah.

The Sultan decided that he must show the Jews that they could not trust their supposed Messiah who was just a common man. He told Sabbatai Zevi that he would set him free for working just one wonder. The Sultan said: "I will have my archers shoot at you with their arrows. If you are really a man who can work wonders for the Jewish people, the arrows will not hurt you. But if you are not their Messiah and just a common man, you will die."

Sabbatai Zevi was afraid to die. He confessed that he was only a common man and dared not face the arrows of the Sultan's archers. The Sultan did not want Sabbatai Zevi to deceive the Jews again. Before the Turkish Messiah was freed from prison, he was forced to become a real Turk and accept the Mohammedan religion.

After that, many of the Jews who had been ready to follow him, knew that he was a false Messiah. But some of them who hated to give up all their hopes, went on believing in him and his power for many years.

THE SULTAN SAID: "I WILL HAVE MY ARCHERS SHOOT AT
YOU WITH THEIR ARROWS"

The Joy of the Torah

"This is the way to study the Torah," runs an old saying of the Jewish people; "Eat bread and salt, drink water by measure, sleep on the earth and live a life of care."

That is how Elijah Gaon, the great rabbi of Wilna, used to study the Torah, the Talmud and other Jewish books. From the time he was a very little boy he loved to study; as he grew older he became so interested in his books that he took very little time to eat or drink, and when he did sit down to his meals he ate only the simplest food. He may have slept in a comfortable bed instead of on the hard floor, but it is certain that he did not go to bed early or sleep late, for he did not want to steal a single moment from his studies.

One day a messenger came to Rabbi Chayim, one of the Gaon's favorite pupils asking him to come to his teacher's house at once. When he reached Elijah Gaon's house he found the rabbi in bed.

"Master," he cried, "are you ill?"

"No, my son," answered Elijah Gaon sadly, "I am not ill in body, but I am sick with care." And he turned his face to the wall.

"He has not eaten for three days," cried the rabbi's wife, who stood by the bed. "And he has hardly slept at all. Soon he will be really sick unless you coax him to take better care of himself."

"Tell me what troubles you, master, and I will do my best to help you," whispered the student, bending over the pillow.

"There are certain passages I cannot understand in the Talmud," answered the wise rabbi. "I have puzzled over them until I am really sick. But, come, let us study together, for 'two are better than one,' and maybe we shall be able to work out what puzzles me."

The two men bent their heads over the heavy book. Hours passed; the sun began to set. The rabbi's wife, who had swept and cleaned the house until it seemed to shine in honor of the "Sabbath Bride," and had blessed the Sabbath lights, went to the window to wait until she saw three stars in the sky; that would mean the beginning of Sabbath Eve. But would her husband and their guest be ready for the Sabbath meal? But she did not dare to disturb them.

It grew too dark for the men to read. Suddenly Elijah Gaon gave a great cry of joy and sprang out of bed. He almost wept for joy; for at last he and his pupil had worked out the meaning of the hard passage in the Talmud.

The rabbi's wife helped him dress in his Sabbath garments. Soon they were all seated round the family table, rejoicing in the coming of the Sabbath Bride. The face of Elijah Gaon shone with happiness; he had often known the "care of the Torah"; now he knew the joy which comes to one who studies the holy books with all his heart.

THE TWO MEN BENT THEIR HEADS OVER THE HEAVY BOOKS

The Boy Who Became the Master
of the Name

In Galicia, there lived long ago a man
and his wife, who wished very much for
a little child. An old story tells that one
day an angel of God came to them, prom-
ising them a child in their old age, who
should be named "Israel," since he would
bring light to the eyes of all Israel. When
the boy was born, the parents named him
Israel and waited anxiously to see whether he would indeed become a great and
wise man in Israel. But they died while
he was still very young.

Little Israel, who was cared for by
some kind people, did not care much for
books. When his teacher tried to explain the Torah to him, he used to steal
away by himself and sit under a tree in
the woods, thinking of many things. As
he grew older, he was given the work of
taking some little children through the
woods to their Hebrew school every day.

112

As they walked through the woods he used to teach them beautiful songs about God, and sing with them.

One day on their way through the forest they met a wolf. When the fathers of the children heard of their danger they said they would not allow them to go through the woods any more until the wolf was killed. But Israel told them not to be afraid. He remembered the story his father had told him just before his death, of the coming of the angel, and God's promise that He would always protect and guide the helpless child. "I am not afraid of the wolf," said Israel.

The next day when he took the children to school and reached the middle of the forest they saw the wolf again, standing in the path, bristling and snarling. Israel raised the club he had brought with him and went fearlessly toward the beast. For a moment the wolf glared at the boy with his wicked, hungry eyes; then his tail drooped between his legs and he ran away, howling in fear. Israel and the other children continued on their way to school. Nobody ever saw the wolf again, and many people believed it was no wolf but some evil spirit sent to prove Israel's courage and teach him to trust in God.

When Israel grew older he became a great leader of the Jewish people, especially in Galicia. Although he had never studied with the other children, but always alone and in secret, he showed great wisdom in all he said and did. But Israel always said that learning was not as important as the Jews had always believed. Up to that time, the rabbis there had taught that an ignorant man who does not understand the Torah cannot know God. But Israel said that loving God was worth more than all the wisdom a man could learn in all the Jewish schools.

Because he could heal the sick through his prayers and seemed to possess such wonderful power, Israel was called Master of the Name (of God). People came to him from all parts of the country; they

ISRAEL RAISED THE CLUB AND WENT TOWARD THE BEAST

were happy if they were allowed even to look upon him. They went back to their own homes to tell of the many wonders he had performed.

Perhaps the greatest thing the Master of the Name did for the Jewish people of his day was to teach them that God was not only in the Holy Books, but that He is everywhere and always lives close to His children. He taught them also that if we really know God we are gay and happy. That is why the Chassidim, Israel's followers, still worship God by dancing and singing happy, merry songs, just as they used to do at the feasts of the great Master of the Name many years ago.

To Seek His Fortune

The watchman at the gates of the great German city of Berlin shook his head crossly at the little boy who stood before him. The child was dirty and dusty, there were holes in his coat, his shoes were almost ready to drop from his feet. His face was pale and sickly; he limped a little and there was an ugly hump upon his bent shoulders.

"You cannot enter the city," said the watchman.

"But I must come in," cried the little boy. "I have walked so far—all the way from Dessau. And I am so tired and hungry that I have not the strength to walk home again."

"We don't want any more beggars in Berlin," growled the watchman.

"But I am not a beggar." The child proudly drew several coins from his pocket. "My father is only a poor scribe;

117

he copies holy books. But he gave me all that he could spare."

The watchman laughed scornfully. "You'd starve in a month. A cripple like you couldn't make your own living. Why did you come to Berlin anyhow?"

"I wanted to study," answered the boy. "My old teacher, Rabbi Frankel, who taught me at Dessau when I was so little and weak that my father used to have to carry me to the school, is now living in Berlin. If I can find him I know that he will teach me again."

"You must be a Jew," said the watchman. "I have seen so many Jews like you, Jews who would rather sit and read a book all day instead of earning money by trade or winning fame as soldiers. But here, you look hungry," he went on, "I have eaten my dinner and there is still a good half-loaf left. My good wife always gives me enough food in a single meal to feed an elephant." He put the loaf into the child's thin hand. "Go on and eat it," he told the boy.

MENDELSSOHN AT THE GATES OF BERLIN

The young traveler sat down upon the ground, took a knife from his pocket and carefully made four notches on the loaf at exact distances from each other. Then he cut off one section, eating it very slowly as though he wanted it to last a long time, picking up the crumbs which fell into his lap as he ate. When the last crumb had disappeared, he thrust the remainder of the loaf into the little bundle of clothes which he had carried at the end of a stick across his shoulders.

"Why did you mark the loaf in four parts?" asked the watchman.

"I was so hungry," answered the boy, "that I was afraid I might eat the whole loaf. But if I am careful I can make it last me four days, a piece for each day. And by that time I may be able to earn a little more."

The watchman laughed. "A boy like you ought to get on. So you've come to Berlin to make your fortune, eh?"

"No, sir, just to study with my old teacher, Rabbi Frankel."

The watchman opened the gate. "Go and find your teacher. But I warn you, you'll have a hard time earning your living in Berlin."

So Moses Mendelssohn, for that was the little boy's name, passed into the city where for many years he starved, and worked hard, and studied. Yet in the end he did make his fortune there—good friends, a loving wife, a comfortable home, and the praises of all Germany. For the ragged little cripple became one of the greatest Jewish scholars, and was honored by both Jews and Christians before he died.

The Man Who Gave Everything

In the days when George Washington led his soldiers against the English troops, there lived in Philadelphia a Jewish broker named Haym Salomon. He had come from Poland while still a young man, had worked hard, and had grown quite wealthy.

The American colonies which were fighting to be free from England were very poor. It was hard for them to borrow money from other countries, because few people believed that America would really win the war. Some people believe that if it had not been for the brokers, Robert Morris, Haym Salomon and several others, this country would never have been able to raise enough money to pay and feed the soldiers who won the war.

Haym Salomon helped at first in other ways. While in New York, he was cap-

SALOMON, SUSPECTED OF AIDING GEN. WASHINGTON, IS CAPTURED

tured by the British who then held the
city; they suspected him of aiding General Washington and imprisoned him in
the old Provost with other military prisoners; here Salomon, because of his
knowledge of many languages, was allowed to act as interpreter and clerk and
was given a great deal of freedom. Before long he was helping the prisoners to
escape; for this the English planned to
hang him, but he escaped just in time and
went to Philadelphia.

From this place he aided his country
with his fortune, never closing his purse
to anybody who came to him for aid. He
not only gave of his own wealth but persuaded both France and Holland to lend
this country money to carry on the war.
When the war was over, although he was
only forty-five, his hard work and cares
had already made him an old man.

Salomon had never asked security for
the money he loaned the government, for
he felt that he could trust his country.
But the war had been long and costly;

when the colonies were free the new United States of America had an empty treasury. There was no money to pay the Jewish broker of Philadelphia.

Salomon had always been generous in all things. He had given to the synagogue of Philadelphia just as freely as to his country and his friends. But now his fortune had dwindled; he had been forced to neglect his own business during the war; merchants who owed him money had failed and could not pay him back. He had nothing left for his own wife and little children.

But Haym Salomon did not complain. Instead, he was glad that he had been able to serve his country.

The City Which Was Never Built

Mordecai Noah wanted to build a city. He was one of the best known Jews in America in his day, known as a statesman, a writer and a speaker. He was very rich and with his money he wanted to help the unhappy Jews of Europe. Why, said Mr. Noah, can't they come to America where they will be well treated?

At that time this country was not as crowded as it is now. Nobody lived in the forests of New York State where the Niagara Falls roared through the silence, except some wild Indians. Mr. Noah had always been friendly with the Indians whom he, like many Christians of his day, believed to belong to the Lost Ten Tribes of Israel. He was sure that the Indians would get on well with the Jews who came to settle in the new city.

So Mordecai Noah sent letters to the

leading Jews all over the world, asking them to send the Jewish people to his new city. Then he invited all the leading people of Buffalo, where he lived, to join with him in a great celebration. There was a great procession with music; afterwards everyone went to one of the churches in Buffalo to hear Mr. Noah speak. Mr. Noah had appointed himself Judge of Israel. He wore a splendid robe of crimson silk trimmed with bands of ermine; no doubt he felt that he was already a king.

There were Indians, too, in the audience. They were puzzled at what Mr. Noah said in his speech, but the white people understood. Mordecai Noah explained that his new city in the wilderness would be a city of refuge for the unhappy Jewish people; that they would find safety there just as Noah and his family had found safety in the Ark during the terrible days of the great flood. And because the Ark had at last come to rest on Mount Ararat, Mordecai Noah planned to call his city Ararat, too. Perhaps, since he was a vain man, he knew that the name of the city would always be connected with his own name, Noah.

Then Mr. Noah caused a monument to be built in the wilderness where he expected the city of Ararat to arise. He wrote more letters to the Jews of Europe; then waited for people to come to his city. But no one came. Some Jews were happy in their own lands; other Jews felt that Mr. Noah was just a foolish, vain man, and would not follow him to the new world. To others, Palestine was the only Promised Land.

So no one came to build the city of Ararat, and at last the monument which Mordecai Noah had raised there, fell into decay. But in the city of Buffalo is still preserved the corner stone of the city which was never built.

THE INDIANS WERE PUZZLED AT WHAT MR. NOAH SAID

Judah Touro, the Man Who Was Everybody's Friend

Judah Touro was the first and one of the greatest Jewish philanthropists who ever lived in America. But perhaps you don't know what a philanthropist is. A philanthropist is a man who loves everybody and is everybody's friend. He is a lover of all mankind. After you hear his story you will know why Judah Touro deserved this name.

Judah was born just about the time the people in America decided that they would not obey the English king any longer. His father was rabbi of the synagogue in Newport, Rhode Island, which is still standing and which is one of the oldest synagogues in the United States. When Mr. Touro died, Judah's good uncle, Moses Michael Hays took charge of him and sent him to school.

Mr. Hays was a merchant, so Judah learned to keep a store, too. While he was still a young man he went south to the city of New Orleans; there he opened

JUDAH TOURO

a shop. He always worked very hard.
Every morning he opened the store himself; every evening he locked the great,
heavy shutters. He always tried never
to be a minute too late or too early.
People in his neighborhood in New
Orleans said that they had no need for a
clock; for Mr. Touro always came past
their doors and returned to his house at
exactly the same moment every night
and morning.

Judah Touro was not only a hard
worker, but he was so honest that everybody trusted him and liked to trade at
his shop. So he became very rich. But
he did not care to use this money for
himself. He never married or had any
children to care for; but as he grew older
he began to look upon everybody who
came to him for help as his own child; he
grew to be a father to all the poor people
of New Orleans and was one of their
best friends.

He gave money to build a home for
orphan boys and girls there; once he
bought a church for some Christian
people of New Orleans and allowed them

to keep it without paying rent until they
were able to buy it back for themselves.

In the same way he helped Jews all
over the United States build synagogues
for his own religion, which was always
very dear to him.

He never forgot the city of Newport
where he was born; he bought the old
Stone Mill there, which some people say
was built by the Norsemen, long before
Columbus came to America. He also
bought the grounds about the Stone Mill
and gave them to the city. This beautiful place in Newport is called Touro
Park till this day.

It would take too long to tell you of all
the good and generous deeds Judah
Touro did during his long, useful life.
But now you know why he was called a
philanthropist; and why since he had no
children to carry on his name, his friends
wrote upon his tomb-stone in the old
cemetery at Newport: "The last of his
name, he inscribed it in the Book of Philanthropy to be remembered forever."

In Far Brazil

Uriah P. Levy had always led a wandering, adventuresome life. As a young man he had known what it was to have the crew of his own vessel mutiny against him; they had taken their youthful captain prisoner and turned him adrift in a small boat on the open sea. But Levy had come safely to land, helped to capture his rebel sailors and see them punished.

He served well in the war of 1812 until he was captured by the English. But when he was released from prison and returned to the United States he was made a lieutenant in the United States Navy. Now, he thought, I can remain in my own country for the rest of my life.

But Levy was of a fiery, quarrelsome nature. In those days men fought duels to settle their quarrels; a duel in which Levy killed his opponent, made him so

134

URIAH P. LEVY

135

many enemies that he had to leave this country. He was dropped from the roll of the United States Navy as captain. When Levy was given some business to take care of in Brazil, he left this country feeling that he had been unjustly treated and would never wish to return to it again.

Now in far Brazil the wanderer began to feel homesick. The emperor of that country, Dom Pedro, admired the American sailor and offered to give him an important position in the Brazilian government. "Stay in my court," said Dom Pedro, "where you may win wealth and honors. I will make you one of the leading men in Brazil."

Then Uriah Levy knew that he wanted to go home. He felt that he would rather live in America as an ordinary citizen, than remain in Brazil where he was promised honor and riches. So he answered the emperor, bowing low before him:

"Your Majesty, I thank you for what you would bestow upon me. But I am still an American citizen and I cannot accept a position under another government."

So Levy returned home. When he reached the United States, he determined to fight for the position which had been taken from him. He managed to have a court appointed to look into the matter of his disgrace; the court decided that he should not have been dropped from the navy. He received back his old position of captain; later he was advanced to the rank of commodore and when the Civil War broke out he was holding the position of flag officer, the highest rank in the American navy at that time.

———◆———

In An English Garden

When Queen Victoria was a young girl, she sometimes left her mother's quiet home in the country to visit near London. Everybody wanted to see the girl who would one day be queen of England. Victoria, who was used to running about her mother's gardens, hated to walk in the streets where everybody turned to look at her.

Then Moses Montefiore, one of the richest and best-loved Jews in England, sent her the key to his own big private garden with a message that she would be free to walk there whenever she pleased, without being disturbed. How the young girl enjoyed walking up and down the well-kept paths, stopping now and then to smell the flowers that grew all about her! Perhaps she asked Moses Montefiore to walk with her sometimes and listened to him with delight when he told her of his travels.

For Moses Montefiore had traveled almost all over the world; he had not gone for his own pleasure but to study the lives of the Jews in different countries and to help them whenever he could. It would be a long story to tell of all the places he visited, all the good he did for his people with his loving heart and great wealth. But the Jews from far and near knew his kindness and never forgot what he did for them.

In Morocco he visited the Sultan, and begged him to be kinder to his Jewish subjects; the Sultan, won by Montefiore's gentleness which no one could resist, promised and was thereafter more merciful to the Jews for his sake. The Sultan of Turkey also promised to be more favorable to the Jews for his sake. Wherever he went, Montefiore gave generously to the poor.

He was one of the first Jews of modern times to help Palestine. He visited the Holy Land seven times and each time he gave a great deal of money to hospitals and homes for the poor. He also planted shrubs and trees in this once beautiful land which had been neglected for so many hundreds of years.

Of course, when they walked in the

garden together Moses Montefiore did
not speak to Victoria of his many chari-
ties. But he may have told her of some
of his exciting adventures in those days
when traveling was really dangerous,
even in civilized England. Once on the
lonely Dover road highway robbers had
shot at the coach in which he and his wife
were riding; in Russia there was the
danger of crossing the river, partly covered with ice; in far Rumania he was
almost killed by an angry mob.

Although she may have forgotten
their talks together, Victoria did not forget Montefiore's lovely garden and the
many happy, quiet hours she had known
there. When she became queen she honored him by making him a knight; after
that he was called Sir Moses Montefiore.

Years later when Sir Moses celebrated
his hundredth birthday a message of
congratulation from his queen made him
very proud and happy. But it must have
made him even prouder and happier to
know that wherever there were Jews, the
scattered sons of Israel prayed that God
might bless the gentle old man for all
the good he had shown to his people.

SIR MOSES MONTEFIORE

An American Rabbi

A little over a hundred years ago there was born in far-off Bohemia a little boy named Isaac M. Wise. His father was a Jewish school teacher and Isaac began to attend his classes at the age of four; at six he began the study of the Talmud, and by the time he was nine, he was so advanced in Hebrew learning, that he was sent to his grandfather's house to live, in order to attend a more advanced school.

When he was still a very young man, Isaac found in a bookstore in the city of Prague a number of old papers and journals from America. He read every one of them over and over again. Years later he said that when he had finished reading these papers he felt like a real American even while he still lived in far-off Bohemia. He made up his mind to come to this country with his family and become an American.

ISAAC M. WISE

143

When he first came to America he tried to support himself by teaching a night school for foreigners like himself. But, as he himself said, he found in a week or two that he had very poor-paying pupils, and they discovered they had a still poorer teacher.

Very soon he became rabbi of a congregation at Albany and teacher of the Hebrew school there. From that time until the end of his long and busy life he served as rabbi and teacher; almost fifty years were spent at Cincinnati, Ohio, where he founded the first college in America for the training of rabbis, called The Hebrew Union College.

Today we do not realize how very important this piece of work was. At that time all of the rabbis in this country had been trained in Europe; many of them were great Hebrew scholars and noble men, but they had not learned American ways and many of them did not know much English and were obliged to preach in German. But the American people wanted rabbis who had studied in America and knew American life.

This school, the Hebrew Union College, grew very fast and has given some of the leading rabbis to America. Rabbi Wise was not only founder of the college, but taught there until his death.

When enough rabbis had graduated they formed under Rabbi Wise's direction the Central Conference of American Rabbis. Their congregations were joined in a group called "The Union of American Hebrew Congregations."

Although a very busy man, Rabbi Wise found time to do a great deal of speaking and writing. He began the Jewish weekly paper "The American Israelite," and was its first editor, and wrote many stories, editorials and poems for it. His books and his printed sermons would fill a long shelf.

No one was ever more generous than Rabbi Wise; he would give the coat from his back to a beggar; his home was always open to the stranger. No matter how busy he was, he always found time to talk to an earnest student in his college, or to make a long journey to another city that he might speak at the dedication of some synagogue. Although modern in his ideas, he was like the rabbis of olden days, always eager to serve the Torah and his fellowman.

Perhaps no one ever described Rabbi Wise any better than his own words did, when he wrote: "I do not wish to be rich nor honored nor recognized nor beloved. I will do my duty." It was the motto for his long and busy and useful life.

The Story of a Dream that Came True

When Theodor Herzl was a school-boy in Austria he may have had dreams just like any other growing boy; but it is not likely that he dreamed his great dream in those days of bringing the homeless Jewish people back to their home-land, Palestine. He was not really interested in Jewish things until years later when he was in Paris during the great Dreyfus trial.

A terrible thing had happened in France. Although the French Jews had long felt at home there, a number of French people hated them so much that they were able to send an innocent man like Captain Dreyfus to prison, just because he was a Jew.

This made Herzl very much ashamed. He said: "Other people have a land of their own; but the Jews have not." Then he began to dream of a home-land for the Jews. Of course he thought of Palestine which the Jews have always remembered so lovingly, although they have been in exile for so many hundreds of years.

Herzl did more than dream of this Old-New Land of Palestine. He wrote many articles and books on Zionism and brought together many people who became Zionists—Jews who were ready to work for the return to Zion (Palestine). At first, many people were against Herzl; even today not everyone agrees with all of his plans. But Herzl went boldly on. He knew that if a man or a people wants anything badly enough it can be brought about.

He visited kings and sultans and statesmen and begged them to help him with his plan to give Palestine back to the Jewish people. He spoke to great gatherings of people. Then he would sit at his desk till morning writing his messages that would reach many others. No work was too hard or too long for him.

THEODOR HERZL

149

But he grew very tired and he was still a young man when he died, worn out by his work for the Jewish people. He did not live to see any of his dream accomplished, but he knew that the work he started would go on.

And the dream of the return to Palestine has indeed come true, perhaps much earlier than Herzl himself had dared to hope.

The English government which has taken possession of Palestine has given the Jewish people perfect freedom in the land of their fathers. Those Jewish people who are still unhappy and badly treated in other countries are going there in great numbers every month; they are learning to be farmers and they are making the land fertile and beautiful once more. Their little children are speaking Hebrew—the old, old language of Palestine—and it is taught to them in their fine, new schools.

The Jews from other parts of the world who are happy in the countries in which they live are also turning to Palestine. Even if they do not care to live there themselves they are sending money to build hospitals and schools there; they are buying ploughs for the farmers; and the school children of America send pennies to buy milk for the babies in Palestine. For the Holy Land has become the Home Land of the Jewish heart.

In Palestine there is a grove called the Herzl Grove. When Jews in far-off America or Germany or Poland wish to celebrate a happy day like a birthday or a marriage, they send money to plant a tree there. These trees make the bare land beautiful; their fruit and wood will help the dwellers in Palestine; they are a living proof that Theodor Herzl's dream will never die.

The Scholar Who Found Hidden Treasure

When Solomon Schechter was a little boy in Roumania he learned to love Hebrew books. He learned to read Hebrew when he was only three years old; at five he was studying the Bible; by the time he was thirteen he was already known for his learning. As he grew older he became more and more interested in his studies. He became a rabbi but he never served in the synagogue; instead, he gave all of his time to studying and teaching.

When Dr. Schechter was teaching in England he had a great adventure. There he was shown a bundle of torn pages which had been found in Palestine. They were so old and stained that it was hard to read the fading Hebrew letters upon them; but Dr. Schechter tried to puzzle out the words. Then he found that one leaf was from the writings of Ben Sira, an old and important

Salomon Schechter

Jewish book. Jewish scholars believed
that this book had at first been written
in Hebrew; but for nearly a thousand
years only Greek copies of the work had
been found.

This lost book was of the greatest in-
terest to students of the Bible. Dr.
Schechter, who had studied Ben Sira's
writings in their Greek form, now
wanted to find the whole Hebrew book
from which the torn page had come.
He believed he might be able to unearth
it in Cairo, Egypt.

So as soon as he could, Solomon
Schechter traveled all the way to Cairo,
Egypt. For one hundred and fifty years
there had been a Genizah there. The
Genizah was a secret place where pious
Jews hid away their holy books which
had become too torn to use, but which
could not be burned or thrown away.
Here the patient scholar worked underground, sorting thousands and thousands
of torn pages. It was dirty and dusty
down there among the musty leaves.
Dr. Schechter really injured his health

through this work; before it was finished, although he was still a young man, he looked very old. But when he returned to England he brought with him boxes and boxes of his treasures. To most people these torn bits from old books would have seemed just worthless scraps; but Dr. Schechter knew that after he had spent long years of study upon them, they would be of the greatest value to anyone who wanted to know more about Jewish books.

When you are older you may want to read for yourself what Dr. Schechter wrote about the treasure he found in Cairo. His books are very learned, but they are not for scholars alone. He had the gift of telling others in a simple and charming way what he himself had studied long years to learn.

For the last years of his life Solomon Schechter was president of the Jewish Theological Seminary of America. This is a school in New York for the training of young rabbis. As the head of this school Dr. Schechter did a great deal to influence American Jewish life through the young rabbis he trained and sent to synagogues all over the land.

He was greatly interested in everything that concerned Jewish life from the hard conditions of the Jews in Russia to the new translation of the Bible, brought out by the Jewish Publication Society of America. Busy as he was, for many years he worked with other scholars on this task of putting the Bible into English. Although the Hebrew language was so dear to him, he believed that if Jews must read the Bible in English, they should have a translation prepared by Jewish scholars, who would understand such work better than even the most learned Christians could.

Solomon Schechter holds an honored place in modern times as a teacher and writer. But he will always be remembered most gratefully for the hidden treasure he found for the Jewish people in the dim, dusty Genizah at Cairo.

The Son of His People

When Israel Zangwill was a little boy in England, he saw many of the sad or jolly sights and met many of the people he afterwards described in his best known book, "Children of the Ghetto." Although the Jews of England are not forced to live behind locked gates any longer, the word **Ghetto** is still used in describing the Jewish quarters of many modern cities. Zangwill grew up in the crowded Ghetto of London; his first important book told the story of what he had seen there.

Few writers of our own time have written more books than Israel Zangwill. He wrote about many things, but everybody likes his Jewish books the best. Some of his books like "Ghetto Comedies" and "They Who Walk in Darkness" were made-up stories; but in "Dreamers of the Ghetto" Zangwill told, as only he could, the life-stories of certain famous Jews. You have already learned of some of them—The Turkish Messiah and Moses Mendelssohn and Spinoza—in this little book. When you are older you will turn Zangwill's pages and see how this prince of story-writers could turn history into a wonderful story book.

Zangwill wrote some verse and essays and a number of plays. Perhaps the most famous one is "The Melting Pot." It tells the story of a Jewish boy who suffered cruelly in Russia, but found a home in America. The boy felt that America was a great melting pot into which all the nations of the world sent their children that they might burn away their old hatreds of each other and come out Americans and brothers. A great many people who had never thought much about this before, began to realize after seeing or reading this play, what America really meant to the Jewish immigrant.

ISRAEL ZANGWILL

Zangwill often left his quiet study to work and fight for the Jewish people. He was one of Herzl's first friends and followers in England. Then Zangwill wondered whether it would not be better for Jews who were not happy in their own countries to settle in other lands, like South America, rather than Palestine. None of these plans worked out well, but Zangwill kept on giving up his strength and time, writing and speaking and working for the Jewish people.

Although the people of England and America honored him as one of the leading English writers, and he had many warm friends outside of his own race, Zangwill never forgot that he was a son of the Jewish people. Perhaps that is why he could write so truthfully and beautifully of the Dreamers and great ones of our race — the humbler men and women who will live forever in the pages of his "Children of the Ghetto."